Losing Lorca showcases a powerful new voice in experimental queer criticism and translation. Olive Esther Kuhn's words—both in translating Lorca's work and writing their own—are precise and exquisite, and their care for both semantic meaning and aesthetic sensibility are evident in each syllable. *Losing Lorca* shows Kuhn's commitment to listening to other voices in imagining a historical queer collective that shifts and bends across time and space.

–Natalie Prizel

Olive Esther Kuhn delivers an exuberant exercise in poetic translation and literary critique. They merge an "ancestral" cultural stream of writers and thinkers with their own experience to explore Queer identities of the past, present and future. Queerness and its socio-political implications is at the soul of *Losing Lorca*, be it Kuhn's translations of Lorca's poetry, or in their own poetic offerings also included, or by the very nature of how the book is structured. *Losing Lorca* is in itself a camera, focused on historical facts filtered through a Queer lens, a potent snapshot of the hopefulness that reparative reading can yield. In Olive Esther Kuhn's unique gaze, there is much to be found.

–Joseph Ivo von Vespri

Kuhn's translations of Federico García Lorca's work deploys reparative rewriting and revelatory experimentation. They draw from Lorca's language ways to envision opportunities for discovery and of "moving beyond." With renewed urgency, Kuhn looks through a lens of Queerness for roadmaps to inspiration within Lorca's poetry. *Losing Lorca* dynamically conveys, in English, the Andalusian poet's mood of eerie dreamscapes and sonority. With light gestures toward connections between the past and what is possible toward an unspecified beyond, Kuhn's writing is both subtle and bold, joyful and suggestive, and replete with hope of Jose Esteban Muñoz's vision of futurity.

–Nicole Caso

We are fortunate indeed to have a guide like Olive Esther Kuhn to accompany us through the recursive Hell/Purgatory/Heaven of Federico García Lorca's eternal surrealist geography. *Losing Lorca* queers translation, composition & commentary with determined courage, telling us old stories & new fables undaunted by a Spanish Civil Guard that still haunts us but cannot (we must believe) dominate our imaginations.

–Eli Goldblatt

Losing Lorca:
a mixtape critique

Design: Christian Ortega
Set in Candida, Henry Morgan Hand, Bell MT and Love Letter TW
Cover Photo: Julia Leiby
Printed in the USA
ISBN 978-1-098315-82-5

Poems by Federico García Lorca translated by Olive Esther Kuhn

FIRST EDITION

www.oliveestherkuhn.com

LOSING

Lorca

a mixtape critique

OLIVE ESTHER KUHN

recto y verso
EDITIONS

CONTENTS

FORWARD

Why the mixtape format?

I spent many hours of my teenage life making 'mixtapes' for my friends. It was the early 2010s, so they weren't
actual mixtapes, but rather mix Compact Discs. Mix CD
didn't sound as good, so I called them mixtapes.

Almost without fail, the recipients of my 'mixtapes'
were female friends for whom I had romantic feelings. I
was not ready to express these feelings openly, so instead
I made mixtapes. I would steal upstairs to my father's
room—a brief detour into masculinity—and take a blank
CD from the stack on his desk. I pirated the songs using a
YouTube-to-mp3 converter, dragged files one-by-one onto
the disc, and wrote out the tracks on a folded scrap of paper. Every step of the process was deliciously secretive.
Closeted, you could say.

Mixtapes and playlists are, to me, a Queer medium.
This is due to personal experience but also to the nature
of the medium: plucking pop songs out of their aesthetic
context and stitching them together into a new pastiche.
My teenage mixtapes were pretty bad: lots of pop punk
and tired grunge. Who knows if the playlists I make now
are any better. I make what makes me happy, and some-
times 'bad' art makes me happy.

The mixtape format of *Losing Lorca* arose out of au-
thorial desperation. I wrote the first iteration of the theory
and translations to satisfy the requirements of an undergraduate thesis. In this academic context, my ideas were

necessarily condensed into dry, inaccessible language and formatting. When Christian Ortega and I decided to publish the piece as experimental literary criticism, I faced the task of slithering out of the thesis shell and into a new form. So I started chopping it up—a translation here, a paragraph on Muñoz here , a historical note here—almost arbitrarily, in the hopes of relocating my voice. In other words, I started making a mixtape.

Eighteen months later I submit to you, not without some misgivings, *Losing Lorca: a mixtape critique*. The songs on each 'side' I chose according to my own appetite. I don't expect you to like them. My own tastes and passions are fleeting. In three years I might not like these songs anymore. I barely speak to the people I made mixtapes for in high school. And it's not that there was some great falling out. Nothing changed except time. The center cannot hold. The wooden desk rots, a leg collapses, and jewel cases cascade into my lap.

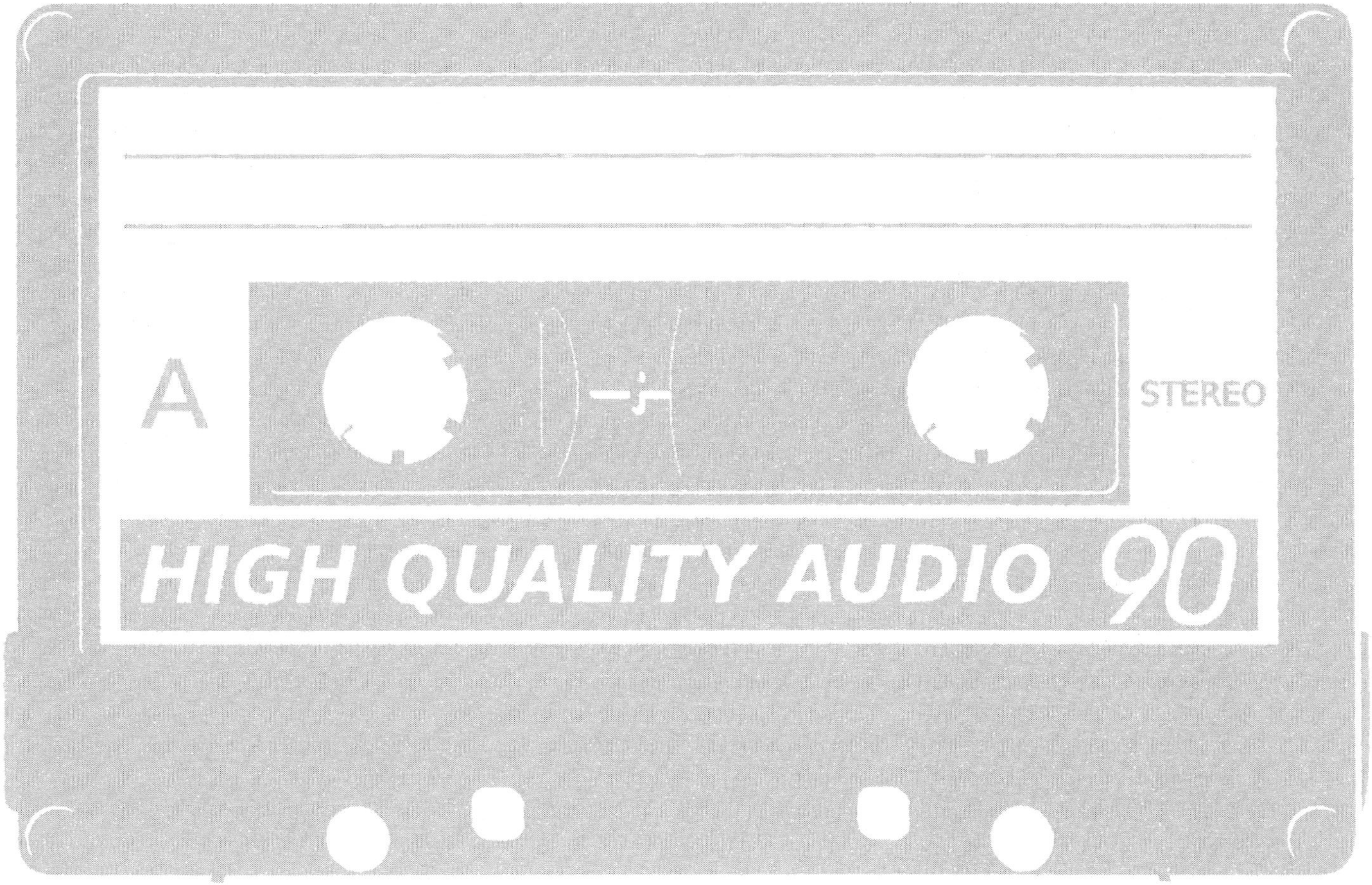
A
STEREO
HIGH QUALITY AUDIO 90

INTRODUCTION

The year is 1936. We are in Andalusia, an autonomous region of southern Spain. The thirty-eight year old poet and dramatist Federico del Sagrado Corazón de Jesús García Lorca is flying high on the successes of his recent tragedies: *Yerma* (1932), *Blood Wedding* (1934) and *The House of Bernarda Alba* (1936). In each play, Lorca dips his fingers into a pool of blood, drawing out a naked silhouette of a Spanish nuclear family. Lorca's portrayals are vivid and haunting: a wife strangles her barren husband, a pregnant woman hangs herself, two suitors duel over a bride neither will live to touch. They are also quite lucrative, making him a celebrated writer for his day.

Lorca's rise to dramaturgical prowess took place in the context of his role as a key member of what we now call the Generation of '27, a group of poets & writers who explored the, then-new, artistic movements of Symbolism, Futurism, and Surrealism. Lorca's rise also took place in the context of a fateful year for Spain's political life; just 5 years prior, King Alfonso XIII fled the country after appointing two unsuccessful prime ministers, and the Second Spanish Republic gained power.

Between '31 and '36, the center-left and center-right political parties play tug of war with the nation. By the spring and summer of 1936, the political landscape has polarized significantly; as land owners, businessmen, Catholics, and the military flocked towards a nationalist right, and a progressive wing of workers, academics, artists and writers align to form a Socialistic left. Indeed, these seasons prove fruitful for both the ultra-right and the writers. Around the same time the poet Luis Cernuda is writing *Reality and Desire*, the Falangistas (fascists) self-organize sporadically across the Spanish map.

In February of 1936, the left elected a national Popular Front. Then the spring set alight and the Spanish Republic sputtered violently. A revolt of right-wing military officers occupying the Canary Islands and Spanish Morocco was led by Francisco Franco. In the following months, the Falangistas gained firm control over Sevilla, Granada and Córdoba. The conflict played out almost comically over Spain's public radio. Imagine today's equivalent of NPR's Terry Gross exclaiming: "Fascists shall not pass! Citizens of Philadelphia, to arms!"

Indeed, the Falangists and the Second Spanish Republic seemed to be competing in a pageantry of chaos. The ruling republican government attempted to compromise with the Falangists, as their own constituents cried traitor. The Falangists, for their part, hungered for more power and operated clandestinely to settle personal vendettas. Executions and assassinations cropped up like poppies.

Lorca's residence was searched thoroughly by Falangists, at least twice, under direct orders of two different generals. By August, Lorca made a fateful decision to hide among *los mismos Falangistas* (the very same Falangists) and fled to the home of poet Luis Rosales. Some of the Rosales brothers were active Falangists, while Luis was merely complicit. Nonetheless, the family took in the wayward Federico. Lorca sang for them, told stories and recited his *romances* as the dogs started to circle. On August 15th, an augury telephoned the Rosales' home to inform Lorca that his brother-in-law, Montesinos, had been executed. On August 16th Ramon Ruiz Alonso, the politician, right-wing activist and typographer by trade, and his men (for lack of a better word) stormed the Rosales home to find Lorca trembling under the family piano. Two civil guardsmen grabbed Lorca by his elbows as Alonso watched from the shadows. The disturbance caused the piano strings to produce a sudden lucid E major chord.

Losing Lorca: a mixtape critique

In the roughly 48 hours that Lorca spent under the watchful eye of the Spanish Civil Guard, the solitude of his mind spun three Cante Jondo songs and an act of a tragicomedy play. These doomed creations were born in silence and reached no audience. Maybe Lorca's cellmates heard his plaintive murmurs? Maybe the guard noticed how Lorca's knuckles twitched, mimicking the motions of pressed piano keys? "What a pervert!" the guard might have said to himself, hoisting up his sagging rifle. Perhaps snippets of dialogue from *The Public* (1930), arguably his least acclaimed play, danced in circles inside Lorca's frantic mind:

THE HORSES:
(Crying)
For just three hundred pesetas.
For two hundred pesetas, for a dish of soup,
for an emptied perfume vial. For your saliva,
for a snipping of your fingernails.

LOS CABALLOS:
(Llorando)
Por trescientas pesetas.
Por doscientas pesetas, por un plato de sopa,
por un frasco de perfume vacío. Por tu saliva,
por un recorte de tus uñas.

These words manifest into air, swirling into an almost forgotten sketch, a self-portrait Lorca had sent to Salvador Dalí after a summer spent on the beach. The letterforms transform into a three-quarter view of Lorca's own face, the words *peseta* the cleft of his forehead, *tus uñas* in the shape of his nose.

In the early morning of August 18th, 1936, unnamed guards take Lorca to an unknown location. His body is framed by the rising sun; the features of his face fade into darkness. Eight authoritarian bullets bury into his body, and he collapses into his own shadow. We do not know where he was shot, as his body was never recovered, but there is a rumor that one Falangist shot his corpse in the buttock *por ser maricon* (for being a faggot). Decades later, Spain's *Caudillo* dictator, Francisco Franco Bahamonde, tried to explain away the assassination of Federico García Lorca as one of the many "accidents of war."

SIDE A:

Queering The Ballads

SUGGESTED TRACKS:
01. *Amar Así*, Bomba Estereo,
02. *True Blue*, Angel Olson & Mark Ronson
03. *Boys Don't Cry*, The Cure
04. *Reconstruye*, Ciénaga
05. *Me Late*, Los Wálters
06. *Hands Up*, Blood Orange
07. *Lately*, Jamila Woods
08. *Lejos*, Sailorfag
09. *HIM*, Sam Smith

Let's take the poem *Ode to Salvador Dalí* as our point of origin. Lorca was 28 years old when he wrote it; 10 years before Lorca's execution by the Spanish Civil Guard, 8 years before Salvador Dalí's expulsion by his fellow Surrealists for not taking a stand against Franco and 2 years before publication of Lorca's *Gypsy Ballads* (1928).

Ode To Salvador Dalí

by Federico García Lorca
(translation by Olive Esther Kuhn)

A rose in the high garden you desire.
A wheel in the lucid syntax of steel.
The mountain bare of impressionist fog.
The grays watching from their last balustrades.

The modern painters in white studios
cut the sterile flower from the square root.
In the Seine's waters a marble iceberg
freezes the windows and parts the ivy.

The man traipses the paved streets.
The crystals dodge their magical reflection.
The government has closed the perfume shops.
The machine makes immortal its binary rhythms.

An absence of forests, screens, and foreheads
roams over the roofs of the old houses.
The air smooths its prism over the sea

and the horizon looms like a great aqueduct.

Sailors who know neither wine nor half-light
decapitate sirens on leaden seas.
The Night, black monument to prudence, holds
the round mirror of the moon in her hand.

Desire for structure seduces us.
Here comes the man who sees with the yellow
ruler. Venus is a white still-life and
the butterfly catchers all run away.

Cadaqués, fulcrum of water and hill,
raises staircases and conceals seashells.
The wooden flutes pacify the air.
An old feral god gives fruits to children.

The fishermen sleep dreamless in the sand.
On high seas a rose serves as their compass.
The virgin horizon of torn kerchiefs
unites the great shards of fish and the moon.

A hard tiara of white brigantines
circles bitter foreheads and sandy hair.
The sirens persuade, but do not sway us.
They'll leave if we show them a glass of fresh water.

Oh, Salvador Dalí, with the olive voice
I do not sing your flawed teenage paintbrush
or your color which woos the color of your time
But I praise your lust for a limited forever.

Untainted soul, you live on fresh marble.
You run from the jungle of absurd forms.
Your fantasy reaches where your hands reach
and you taste the sea's sonnet at your window.

The world holds deafened half-light and chaos
in the foreground which we humans frequent

But now the stars, concealing whole landscapes
reveal the perfect scheme of their orbits.

Elapsed time pools and takes the numeric
form of a century and another.
And defeated, trembling Death takes refuge
in the tiny circle of the present.

Holding your pallet, gunshot in one wing,
you invoke the light in the olive tree.
Broad light of Minerva, scaffold builder,
where inexact dream flowers have no home.

You invoke the ancient light which lingers on
his forehead, falling neither to his mouth
nor his heart. Light which Baco's precious grape
vines fear and the lawless force of bending water.

You are right to put flags of warning
on the dark border that gleams in the night
You won't have your paintings' forms be softened
by an unforeseen cloud's ghostly cotton.

The fish in its fishbowl, the bird in its cage.
You don't invent them in the sea or sky.
You style or copy, having observed
with honest pupils their agile bodies.

You love a defined and exact matter
upon which no fungus can grow. You love
the architecture built upon the nothing.
and you see the flag as a simple joke.

The steel compass recites its short, elastic verse.
Unknown islands argue with the sphere.
The straight line speaks of its upward struggle
and the wise crystals sing their geometries.

But remember the rose in your garden.

Always the rose, to our north and our south.
Calm and distilled like a blind statue, not
knowing what chaos it causes below.
Pure rose free of artifice and sketches
which opens our smiles' tenuous wings.
(a pinned-down butterfly meditates flight).
Rose of balance with no sought-out wounds.
Always the rose!

Oh, Salvador Dalí with the olive voice!
I say what you and your paint say to me.
I do not praise your flawed teenage paintbrush
but I sing the firm aim of your arrows.

I sing the Catalan lights of your work,
your love for possible explanations.
I sing your astronomic, tender heart,
of French playing cards without injury.

I sing your lust for the statue you pursue.
The fear of the feelings you meet in the streets.
I sing of the siren that sings to you
on a bicycle of corals and shells.

But, above all, I sing a common thought
that unites us in dark and golden hours.
The light which blinds the eyes is not Art.
What wins out is friendship, love, or fencing.

Before the portrait you patiently draw,
Teresa's breast, the sleepless complexion,
the curls of Matilde the ungrateful,
is our friendship shown as a game of goose.

Let blood-tinted fingerprints scratch the heart
of golden eternal Catalonia.
Stars like hawk-less fists illuminate you,
as your painting and your life flourish.

Losing Lorca: a mixtape critique

Don't watch the hourglass with membranous wings
nor the severe allegorical scythe.
Dress and undress your paintbrush in the air
forever, facing an ocean of ships and sailors.

⏮ ■ ▶ ⏸ ● ⏭

Oda A Salvador Dalí
by Federico García Lorca

Una rosa en el alto jardín que tu deseas.
Una rueda en la pura sintaxis del acero.
Desnuda la montaña de niebla impresionista.
Los grises oteando sus balaustradas últimas.

Los pintores modernos, en sus blancos estudios,
cortan la flor aséptica de la raíz cuadrada.
En las aguas del Sena un iceberg de mármol
enfría las ventanas y disipa las yedras.

El hombre pisa fuerte las calles enlosadas.
Los cristales esquivan la magia del reflejo.
El Gobierno ha cerrado las tiendas de perfume.
La máquina eterniza sus compases binarios.

Una ausencia de bosques, biombos y entrecejos
yerra por los tejados de las casas antiguas.
El aire pulimenta su prisma sobre el mar
y el horizonte sube como un gran acueducto.

Marineros que ignoran el vino y la penumbra
decapitan sirenas en los mares de plomo.
La Noche, negra estatua de la prudencia, tiene
el espejo redondo de la luna en su mano.

Un deseo de formas y límites nos gana.
Viene el hombre que mira con el metro amarillo.
Venus es una blanca naturaleza muerta

y los coleccionistas de mariposas huyen.

Cadaqués, en el fiel del agua y la colina,
eleva escalinatas y oculta caracolas.
Las flautas de madera pacifican el aire.
Un viejo dios silvestre da frutas a los niños.

Sus pescadores duermen, sin ensueño, en la arena.
En alta mar les sirve de brújula una rosa.
El horizonte virgen de pañuelos heridos
junta los grandes vidrios del pez y de la luna.

Una dura corona de blancos bergantines
ciñe frentes amargas y cabellos de arena.
Las sirenas convencen, pero no sugestionan,
y salen si mostramos un vaso de agua dulce.

¡Oh Salvador Dalí, de voz aceitunada!
No elogio tu imperfecto pincel adolescente
ni tu color que ronda la color de tu tiempo,
pero alabo tus ansias de eterno limitado.

Alma higiénica, vives sobre mármoles nuevos.
Huyes la oscura selva de formas increíbles.
Tu fantasía llega donde llegan tus manos,
y gozas el soneto del mar en tu ventana.

El mundo tiene sordas penumbras y desorden,
en los primeros términos que el humano frecuenta.
Pero ya las estrellas ocultando paisajes,
señalan el esquema perfecto de sus órbitas.

La corriente del tiempo se remansa y ordena
en las formas numéricas de un siglo y otro siglo.
Y la Muerte vencida se refugia temblando
en el círculo estrecho del minuto presente.

Al coger tu paleta, con un tiro en un ala,
pides la luz que anima la copa del olivo.

Ancha luz de Minerva, constructora de andamios,
donde no cabe el sueño ni su flora inexacta.
Pides la luz antigua que se queda en la frente,
sin bajar a la boca ni al corazón del hombre.
Luz que temen las vides entrañables de Baco
y la fuerza sin orden que lleva el agua curva.

Haces bien en poner banderines de aviso,
en el límite oscuro que relumbra de noche.
Como pintor no quieres que te ablande la forma
el algodón cambiante de una nube imprevista.

El pez en la pecera y el pájaro en la jaula.
No quieres inventarlos en el mar o en el viento.
Estilizas o copias después de haber mirado
con honestas pupilas sus cuerpecillos ágiles.

Amas una materia definida y exacta
donde el hongo no pueda poner su campamento.
Amas la arquitectura que construye en lo ausente
y admites la bandera como una simple broma.

Dice el compás de acero su corto verso elástico.
Desconocidas islas desmienten ya la esfera.
Dice la línea recta su vertical esfuerzo
y los sabios cristales cantan sus geometrías.

Pero también la rosa del jardín donde vives.
¡Siempre la rosa, siempre, norte y sur de nosotros!
Tranquila y concentrada como una estatua ciega,
ignorante de esfuerzos soterrados que causa.

Rosa pura que limpia de artificios y croquis
y nos abre las alas tenues de la sonrisa.
(Mariposa clavada que medita su vuelo.)
Rosa del equilibrio sin dolores buscados.
¡Siempre la rosa!

¡Oh Salvador Dalí de voz aceitunada!

Olive Esther Kuhn

Digo lo que me dicen tu persona y tus cuadros.
No alabo tu imperfecto pincel adolescente,
pero canto la firme dirección de tus flechas.

Canto tu bello esfuerzo de luces catalanas,
tu amor a lo que tiene explicación posible.
Canto tu corazón astronómico y tierno,
de baraja francesa y sin ninguna herida.

Canto el ansia de estatua que persigues sin tregua
el miedo a la emoción que te aguarda en la calle.
Canto la sirenita de la mar que te canta
montada en bicicleta de corales y conchas.

Pero ante todo canto un común pensamiento
que nos une en las horas oscuras y doradas.
No es el Arte la luz que nos ciega los ojos.
Es primero el amor, la amistad o la esgrima.

Es primero que el cuadro que paciente dibujas
el seno de Teresa, la de cutis insomne,
el apretado bucle de Matilde la ingrata,
nuestra amistad pintada como un juego de oca.

Huellas dactilográficas de sangre sobre el oro
rayen el corazón de Cataluña eterna.
Estrellas como puños sin halcón te relumbren,
mientras que tu pintura y tu vida florecen.

No mires la clepsidra con alas membranosas,
ni la dura guadaña de las alegorías.
Viste y desnuda siempre tu pincel en el aire,
frente a la mar poblada con barcos y marinos.

⏮ ■ ▶ ⏸ ● ⏭

There are several reasons why Federico García Lorca was executed. He was a poet, he was gay, he fraternized with Communists and he wrote 'subversive' verse and plays. Maybe Franco simply ordered that particular squad to kill that *maricon*? Maybe a guard found his coffee too weak and took his rage out on Lorca? Fascism is funny like that. But I'm getting ahead of myself.

In *Gypsy Ballads (Romancero Gitano)*, published in 1928, Lorca uses the form of a traditional Spanish ballad to weave chromatic tales of gypsies, saints, and the violent Civil Guard (more on this soon). Upon reading the ballads, Lorca's good friend Salvador Dalí wrote a letter to the young poet. The letter[1], marked by Dali's distinctive disregard for spelling and grammar, delivers a pointed but rambling critique of the book. Dalí claims that the ballads, for all their fantasy and enigma, are too attached to reality. He begs Lorca to abandon his rhyme schemes, arguing that the medieval form of *el romance* renders his voice stuffy and irrelevant. He urges Lorca, instead, towards the realm of Surrealism. In his comments on *Gypsy Ballads*, Dalí seems to be saying the work strays from Lorca's true nature: the dark and the animal.

No sooner does Dalí level these critiques than he abruptly changes tone and addresses Lorca as a lover. In his peculiar voice, riddled with flagrant misspellings and grammatical flukes, Dalí espouses his deep affection for Lorca: for his body, his hair, his eyes, his very heart. For context, the two men did share an intimate relationship. The extent to which Dalí and Lorca sexually consummated their relationship remains unknown, and I don't think it really matters. I am more interested in the double-edged sword that Dalí's letter to Lorca presents: to ignore the homoerotic content and read it only as straightforward critique is irresponsible. But it's equally irresponsible to overlook Dalí's literary points and interpret the letter as a correspondence between two lovers. Dalí's letter demands to be read as literature—but literature within a Queer context.

The word Queer is a world within a syllable. It is an indefinite, possibly undefinable word. Every time a Queer person lives, we reconstitute the word. In the most layman's terms, to be Queer means to not be heterosexual,

[1] The letter is printed in full in Ian Gibson's biography *Federico García Lorca: De Fuente Vaqueros a Nueva York.*

but there are many ways to not be something. **I am not an electrician named Steve**, but that doesn't tell you very much about me.

One definition of Queerness which I find particularly illuminating is put forward by Jose Esteban Muñoz in his masterful book *Cruising Utopia: the then and now of queer futurity* (2009). Muñoz posits that to be Queer is to both live in the present and the future, between the polarity of the absurdity of the present and the possibilities of the future. Queerness can be utopian, not in a sense of inhabiting an already perfect world, but in searching for alternative realities. Muñoz's Queer utopia does not diverge from reality. Muñoz's Queerness rewrites, constructs, resees reality.

One of my favorite things about reading literature through a Queer lens is the possibility of reparative reading.[2] By this I mean not only unearthing the Queer suffering embedded in so much writing, but also shining light on the Queer joy that pulsates beneath the surface of literature and history. Reparative reading means, more or less, reading to repair. But who or what is the reader repairing? When I translated *Ode to Salvador Dalí*, I made the choice to underscore the sexual nature of Lorca's desire. This choice felt reparative. Not because I was somehow repairing the text, but because the process was healing for me, the translator.

Letter To Salvador Dalí
by Olive Esther Kuhn

Dear Salvadorcito,

You tell Federiquito that his ballads are too emotional. I have some things to tell you. First argument: they're fucking ballads. Or, in Spanish, romances. Romance, romancero, it's not difficult. Second argument: Is the river too wet for you as well,

[2] Put forward by Eve Kosofsky Sedgwick in *Touching Feeling*.

Salvadorcito? Are the men too male? Is the sex too sexual? Third argument: What compels you to to tell your lover of several years that his work is too emotional? What are you afraid of?

When I say lover, I mean: that you spent a green summer together in Cadaqués, that you introduced Lorca to your little sister, to your parents. That they loved him like an adopted son. That you painted him a thousand times with your very avantgarde brush. In fact the paint brush was so avantgarde that it was your body. Maybe. I don't know what happened during those nights of eternal return, when you drank gin like milk and you stayed up all night. I don't care what happened in "reality," this word you distrust so deeply. I don't care what your bodies did or did not do. What I do care about is what he wrote, and what you wrote.

Let's talk about reality, Salvadorcito. In the letter you wrote to Lorca, you say that his poetry is too traditional--too real. There are horses and riders and rhyme schemes. Not a single clock melts. And this, you can't seem to bear. What compassion you have for clocks. And what shame you have for human beings.

So I'd rather talk about your ex-companion's overwrought, but very honest, verses. "Oh, Salvador Dalí with the olive voice! I speak what you and your paint say to me. I do not praise your flawed teenage paintbrush but I sing the firm aim of your arrows." He published this in La Revista de Occidente in 1929, in the twilight of a gilded decade: "The light which blinds the eyes is not Art. Rather it is friendship, love, or fencing."

This too he wrote, published, declared in every corner of Andalusia. I'll ask you again, Salvadorcito: What were you afraid of?

Dear Salvadorcito, Federico García Lorca was

executed by the Spanish Civil Guard on August eighteenth, 1936. He was thirty-eight years old. You hid in America from the war, then returned to Spain like a real Andalusian dog. You lived in comfort beneath Franco's fist. You died in 1989 at the age of eighty-five while listening to Tristan and Isolde, your favorite album in the entire world. Your body is buried in the crypt beneath your own museum.

It is now believed that Federiquito's body was buried nameless outside the village of Alfacar, but we still don't know for sure.

-O.E.K.

ı◄◄ ■ ► ıı ● ►►ı

Carta A Salvador Dalí
by Olive Esther Kuhn

Querido Salvadorcito,

Le dices a Federiquito que sus romances son demasiados emocionales. Yo tengo algunas cosas que decirte. Argumento primero: son malditos romances. Romancero, romance, no es difícil. Además del pecado de emoción, los romances, dices tú, son demasiado andaluces. Argumento segundo: ¿Es demasiado mojado el río también, Salvadorcito? ¿Es demasiado hombre el hombre? ¿Demasiado sexual el sexo? Argumento tercero: ¿Y cómo es que le dirás a tu amante de tantos años que su obra es demasiado emocional? ¿De qué tienes miedo?

Cuando yo digo amante, yo quiero decir: que ustedes pasaron juntos un verano verde en las playas de Cadaqués, que le presentaste Lorca a tu hermana pequeña, a tus padres. Que ellos le amaban como un hijo adoptado. Que lo pintó mil veces con el pincel muy, muy vanguardista. De hecho era un pincel tan vanguardista que era tu cuerpo mismo. Tal vez. No se sabe qué pasó realmente durante estas noches del eterno retorno, cuando bebieron ginebra como leche y trasnocharon. Y a mí no me importa nada qué pasó en "realidad," esa palabra en que te desconfias tanto. A mi no me importa qué hicieron o no hicieron sus cuerpos. Lo que sí me importa es lo que él escribió, y lo que escribiste tú.

Hablamos acerca de la realidad, Salvadorcito. En la carta que le escribiste a Lorca, dices que su poesía es demasiado tradicional--demasiado real. Hay caballos y jinetes y esquemas de rima. Ningún reloj se derrite. Qué compasión tienes por los relojes. Y qué verguenza por los seres humanos.

Entonces prefiero enfocarme en los versos ingenuos, pero muy honestos, de su examigo: "¡Oh, Salvador Dalí de voz aceitunada! Digo lo que me dicen tu persona y tus cuadros. No alabo tu imperfecto pincel adolescente, pero canto la firme dirección de tus flechas." Esto lo publicó en La Revista de Occidente en 1929, al crepúsculo de la década dorada. "No es el Arte la luz que nos ciega los ojos. Es primero el amor, la amistad o la esgrima."

Esto también lo escribió, lo publicó, lo declaró, en cada rincón de Andalucía. Te pregunto otra vez, Salvadorcito: ¿De que tienes miedo?

Querido Salvadorcito, Federico García Lorca fue ejecutado por la Guardia Civil de España el 18 de agosto, 1936. Tenía treinta y ocho años. Tú huiste de la guerra en los Estados Unidos, pues regresaste a España como un verdadero perrón de Andalucía. Viviste cómodamente bajo el puño de Franco. Te moriste en 1989 a la edad de ochenta y cinco años mientras escuchabas a Tristan y Isolde, tu álbum favorito en todo el mundo. Tu cuerpo está enterrado en la cripta bajo su propio museo.

Ahora pensamos que el cuerpo de Federiquito fue enterrado sin nombre fuera del pueblo de Alfacar, pero no se sabe por cierto.

-O.E.K.

I◀ ■ ▶ II ● ▶I

Before we go any further, I want to break down the title *Gypsy Ballads*. Within the first word, Gypsy *(Gitano)*, Lorca is referring to the Romani people who live in their shared homeland of Andalusia. I'm by no means an expert on Romani history, but I will say that gypsies migrated to Spain from India via Northern Africa between 900 and 1400 AD. As King Fernando and Queen Isabella were expelling the Moors and the Jews from Spain in 1492 *(Columbus sailed the ocean blue...)* to solidify Spain as a Catholic state, the gypsies were targeted as well. Still, the gypsy culture and people continued to thrive in Spain, Andalusia especially, despite substantial repression and stigma (more on this soon).

The second word, Ballads *(el romance)*, historically is a popular form of Spanish storytelling which consist of an indefinite number of 8 syllable lines. All of the even-numbered lines end in bisyllabic assonant rhyme (the vowels rhyme but the consonants don't). As a result each poem is marked by the recurrence of specific vowel sounds. For example, in Lorca's poem *Sleepwalking Ballad* from *Gypsy Ballads* the 2nd, 4th, 6th, and 8th lines end, respectively, in *ramas, montaña, baranda,* and *mirarlas.* For the record, this rhyming scheme is more possible in the Spanish language than in English. Ill-advised English language interpretations have led, I believe, to some cringeworthy versions of Lorca's ballads. I tried myself, resulting in quite awful poetics. I eventually found a way to retain Lorca's lyricism in a more comparable metrical scheme, using 6 syllable lines instead of 8, in the following:

Sleepwalking Ballad

by Federico García Lorca
(translation by Olive Esther Kuhn)

Green, how I want you green.
Green the wind, branches of green.
The boat upon the sea,
the horse in the mountain.
Shadows on her waist, she
dreams on the balcony.
Green skin, hair of green,
and eyes of cold silver.
Green, how I want you green.
Beneath the gypsy moon,
the things are watching her
and she cannot watch back.

Green, how I want you green.
Monstrous stars of frost
arrive with a shadow fish
that opens the path to dawn.
The fig tree rubs its branches
sandpaper in the wind.
The hill, a feral cat,
prickles its acrid pelt.
But, who will come? and where from?
she repeats on her balcony.
Green skin and hair of green
dreaming in the bitter sea.
-Brother, let me exchange
my horse for your estate,
my saddle for your mantle,
your mirror for my knife.
Brother, I've been bleeding
since the ports of Cabra.
-If I were able, boy,
this exchange would be made.
But I am not myself
and my house is no longer my house.

-Brother, I want to die
decently in my bed.
A steel bed, if I can,
with fine Dutch linen sheets.
See my wound? It stretches
from my throat to my chest.
-Three hundred dark roses
bloom on your white shirt-front.
Your blood oozes and pools
all around your bandage.
But I am not myself
and my house is no longer my house.
-Let me ascend, at least,
to the top of the stairs.
The handrails of the moon
echo in the water.

And so the two men climb
up to the highest stair
leaving a train of blood
leaving a stain of tears.
Hanging lanterns of tin
trembled in the rafters.
A thousand crystal tambourines
wounded the early morning.

Green, how I want you green.
Green the wind, branches of green.
The two men ascended.
The great wind left a strange
taste in the mouth of mint,
of honey and basil.
-Brother, where is she, tell me!
Where is your bitter girl?
How many times she waited for you,
and how many more she would have!
A fresh face and black hair
on this green balcony!
Upon the cistern's lips

the gypsy girl was swaying.
Green flesh, hair of green,
with eyes of cold silver.
The moon in an icicle's form
suspends her upon the water.
The night became intimate
with the little plaza.
Drunken civil guardsmen
were banging on the door.
Green, how I want you green.
Green the wind, branches of green.
The boat on the sea,
The horse in the mountain.

|◀ ■ ▶ ‖ ● ▶|

Romance Sonámbulo

by Federico García Lorca

Verde que te quiero verde.
Verde viento. Verdes ramas.
El barco sobre la mar
y el caballo en la montaña.
Con la sombra en la cintura,
ella sueña en su baranda,
verde carne, pelo verde,
con ojos de fría plata.
Verde que te quiero verde.
Bajo la luna gitana,
las cosas la están mirando
y ella no puede mirarlas.

Verde que te quiero verde.
Grandes estrellas de escarcha
vienen con el pez de sombra
que abre el camino de alba.
La higuera frota su viento
con la lija de sus ramas;

el monte, gato garduño,
riza sus pitas tan agrias.
¿Pero, quién vendrá? ¿Y por dónde?
Sigue en su baranda,
verde carne, pelo verde,
soñando en la mar amarga.
-Compadre, quiero cambiar
mi caballo por su casa,
mi montura por su espejo,
mi cuchillo por su manta.
Compadre, vengo sangrando
desde los puertos de Cabra.
- Si yo pudiera, mocito,
este trato se cerraba.
Pero yo ya no soy yo,
ni mi casa es ya mi casa.
-Compadre, quiero morir
decentemente en mi cama.
De acero, si puede ser,
con las sábanas de holanda.
¿No ves la herida que tengo
desde el pecho a la garganta?
-Trescientas rosas morenas
lleva tu pechera blanca.
Tu sangra rezuma y huele
alrededor de tu faja.
Pero yo ya no soy yo,
ni mi casa es ya mi casa.
-Dejadme subir al menos
hasta las altas barandas.
Barandales de la luna
por donde retumba el agua

Ya suben los dos compadres
hacia las altas barandas.
Dejando un rastro de sangre.
Dejando un rastro de lágrimas.
Temblaban en los tejados
farolillos de hojalata.

Mil panderos de cristal
herían la madrugada.

Verde que te quiero verde,
verde viento, verdes ramas.
Los dos compadres subieron.
El largo viento dejaba
en la boca un raro gusto
de hiel, de menta, y de albahaca.
¡Compadre! ¿Dónde está, dime,
dónde está tu niña amarga?
¡Cuántas veces te esperó!
Cuántas veces te esperara,
cara fresca, negro pelo,
en esta verde baranda!

Sobre el rostro de aljibe,
se mecía la gitana.
Verde carne, pelo verde,
con ojos de fría plata.
Un carámbano de luna
la sostiene sobre el agua.
La noche se puso íntima
con una pequeña plaza.
Guardias civiles borrachos
en la puerta golpeaban.
Verde que te quiero verde.
Verde viento. Verdes ramas.
El barco sobre la mar.
Y el caballo en la montaña.

|◄◄ ■ ► ❚❚ ● ►►|

This poem has been analyzed to death in the nine-
ty-two years since its publication. I will not use my limited
time here to interpret every line. I do want to call attention, however, to the line in the final stanza *Drunken civil
guardsmen were banging on the door.* Here, 'civil guards-

men' refers to *la guardia civil*, the rural law enforcement body that 'protected' Andalusia. Conflicts between the civil guards and the gypsies, *los gitanos*, pervade the ballads (Lorca sides with the gypsies, although, as you will soon see, they do not always win).

I say 'side with' because Lorca himself was not a gypsy. He grew up among Gypsy people, and was heavily invested in gypsy culture and art, but he and his family belonged to a more whitewashed and wealthy Spanish class. From our historical standpoint, Lorca's interest or obsession with gypsy culture feels exploitative. What's ironic is that art forms one might now consider essentially Spanish, such as flamenco music and dance, started as gypsy traditions. Very broadly speaking, the early 20th century marks the assimilation of these traditions as "Spanish" culture.

Does this absorption constitute acceptance, erasure, or some combination thereof? I am in no position to decide. What I can say is that, in Lorca's poetic and historical context, his choice to situate *los gitanos* as the protagonists of a *romancero* was a bold one. The *romance*, as we've established, is a quintessentially Spanish form. By mooring the *romance* to an 'outsider' class Lorca subverts this established form. Thus we can read the work as a rejection of an emerging nationalist Spanish identity.

Meanwhile, the subversive nature of Lorca's ballads is juxtaposed by faithful adherence to the metrical and rhyming form of the ballad. The entire text of *Romancero Gitano* takes place within the confines of the *romance's* rhythmic and metrical schemes: in this way the form allows the content to float in a harmonic dreamspace. The sound of Lorca's ballads divests them from the quotidian world of unrhymed speech in a new and separate world. Tradition and the future fused. It's in these simultaneous actions of pushing away and also demanding a new reality where I locate Muñoz's concept of Queerness within Lorca's work (as we've established, Muñoz identifies Queerness as an art that entertains both a dreamspace and a disenchanted reality).

In the following ballad, Lorca narrates the destruction of a gypsy encampment by the Spanish Civil Guard. While mourning the loss of this gypsy enclave Lorca, in his mind, reconstructs the community and presents it in the form of a dreamscape.

Ballad Of The Spanish Civil Guard

by Federico García Lorca
(translation by Olive Esther Kuhn)

Black are their horses.
Their horseshoes are black.
Stains of the ink and wax
ripple on their capes.
They do not cry, because
their skulls are made of lead.
Down the highway come the men
with patent-leather soles.
Hunchbacked, nocturnal,
wherever they haunt,
they bring dark rubber silence
and fear like grains of sand.
They go where they like
hiding in their minds
a vague astronomy
of insecure pistols.

Oh, city of gypsies!
Flags in every corner.
The moon and the pumpkin,
the sweet preserved cherries.
Oh, city of gypsies!
Who could see you and forget?
City of ache and musk,
a cinnamon tower city.
When the night was falling,
night what a night of nights,
The gypsies in their smithies
were forging suns and arrows.

A badly-wounded horse
was calling at all the doors.
Glass roosters were singing
by Jerez de la Frontera.
The wind turns the corner,
naked and surprised
in the night, oh silver night,
night what a night of nights.
The Virgin and San José
lost their castanets
and search among the gypsies
to see if they can find them.
The Virgin comes dressed
like a mayor's wife
in chocolate paper
with almond necklaces.
San José waves his arms
beneath a silken cape.
Behind comes Pedro Domecq
with three Sultans from Persia.
The half moon was dreaming
of a stork's ecstasy.
Battle standards and lanterns
colonize the rooftops.
In the mirrors, sob
dancers with no hips.

Water and shadow, shadow and water
by Jerez de la Frontera.

Oh, city of gypsies!
Flags in every corner.
Extinguish your green lights, for
the authorities are upon you.
Oh, city of the gypsies!
Who could see you and forget?
Leave her, far from the sea,
with no combs to part her hair.

Losing Lorca: a mixtape critique

Two-by-two they advance
toward the celebrating city.
A whisper of immortelle flowers
invades their ammunition pouches.
Two-by-two they advance,
a double uniform nocturn.
The sky to in their eyes resembles
a glass cabinet of spurs.

The city, free of fear,
was opening all its doors.
Forty civil guards
enter them ready to sack.
The clocks all stopped
and the cognac in the bottles
disguised itself as November
so as not to raise suspicion.
Great cries flew up
through the weather vanes.
The sabers cut the wind, which
the horses' hooves then trample.
Through the half-lit streets,
flee the old gypsy women.
with their drowsy horses
and pigskins full of coins.
Up the breakneck street
the sinister capes rise
leaving behind fleeting
whirlwinds of scissors.

At the gate of Belén,
the gypsies assemble.
San José, covered in wounds,
lays a shroud over a maiden.
Piercing missiles sounded
doggedly the whole night through.
The Virgin cures children
with spittle from a star.
But the Civil Guard advances,

setting fire to homes,
where, young and naked,
imagination burns.
Rosa of the Camborios
moans at the foot of her door
with her two severed breasts
placed on a tray.
And other girls were running
pursued by their braids
as, in the air around them,
roses of black gunpowder burst.
When all of the roofs
were notches in the earth,
the sunrise cradled its shoulders
in the profile of a great stone.

Oh, city of the gypsies!
The Civil Guard departs
through a tunnel of silence
as the flames encroach upon you.
Oh, city of gypsies!
Who could see you and forget?
Let them search my brow for you.
A game of moon and sand.

⏮ ■ ▶ ❚❚ ● ⏭

Romance de la Guardia Civil de España
by Federico García Lorca

Los caballos negros son.
Las herraduras son negras.
Sobre las capas relucen
manchas de tinta y cera.
Tienen, por eso no lloran,
de plomo las calaveras.
Con el alma de charol

vienen por la carretera.
Jorobados y nocturnos,
por donde animan ordenan
silencios de goma oscura
y miedos de fino arena.
Pasan, si quieren pasar,
y ocultan en la cabeza
una vaga astronomía
de pistolas inconcretas.

¡Oh, ciudad de los gitanos!
En las esquinas, banderas.
La luna y la calabaza
con las guindas en conserva.
¡Oh, ciudad de los gitanos!
¿Quién te vio y no te recuerda?
Ciudad de dolor y almizcle,
con las torres de canela.
Cuando llegaba la noche
noche que noche nochera,
los gitanos en sus fraguas
forjaban soles y flechas.
Un caballo malherido
llamaba a todas las puertas.
Gallos de vidrio cantaban
por Jerez de la Frontera.
El viento vuelve desnudo
la esquina de la sorpresa,
en la noche platinoche,
noche que noche nochera.

La Virgen y San José
perdieron sus castañuelas,
y buscan a los gitanos
para ver si las encuentran.
La Virgen viene vestida
con un traje de alcaldesa
de papel de chocolate
con sus collares de almendras.

San José mueve sus brazos
bajo una capa de seda.
Detrás va Pedro Domecq
con tres sultanes de Persia.
La media luna soñaba
un éxtasis de cigüeña.
Estandartes de faroles
invaden las azoteas.
Por los espejos sollozan
bailarinas sin caderas.

Agua y sombra, sombra y agua
por Jerez de la Frontera.

¡Oh, ciudad de los gitanos!
En las esquinas, banderas.
Apaga tus verdes luces
que viene la benemérita.
¡Oh, ciudad de los gitanos!
¿Quién te vio y no te recuerda?
Dejadla lejos del mar
sin peines para sus crenchas.

Avanzan de dos en fondo
a la ciudad de la fiesta.
Un rumor de siemprevivas
invade las cartucheras.
Avanzan de dos en fondo.
Doble nocturno de tela.
El cielo se les antoja
una vitrina de espuelas.

La ciudad, libre de miedo,
multipliciaba sus puertas.
Cuarenta guardias civiles
entran a saco por ellas.
Los relojes se pararon
y el coñac de las botellas
se disfrazó de Noviembre

para no infundir sospechas.
Un vuelo de gritos largos
se levantó en las veletas.
Los sables cortan las brisas
que los cascos atropellan.
Por las calles de penumbra,
huyen las gitanas viejas,
con los caballos dormidos
y las orzas de moneda.
Por las calles empinadas,
suben las capas siniestras,
dejando detrás fugaces
remolinos de tijeras.

En el portal de Belén
los gitanos se congregan.
San José, lleno de heridas,
amortaja a una doncella.
Tercos fusiles agudos
por toda la noche suenan.
La Virgen cura a los niños
con salivilla de estrella.
Pero la Guardia Civil
avanza sembrando hogueras,
donde joven y desnuda
la imaginación se quema.
Rosa de los Camborios
gime sentada en su puerta
con sus dos pechos cortados
puestos en una bandeja.
Y otras muchachas corrían
perseguidas por sus trenzas,
en un aire donde estallan
rosas de pólvora negra.
Cuando todos los tejados
eran surcos en la tierra,
el alba meció sus hombros
en largo perfil de piedra.

¡Oh, ciudad de los gitanos!
La Guardia Civil se aleja
por un túnel de silencio
mientras las llamas te cercan.
¡Oh, ciudad de los gitanos!
¿Quién te vio y no te recuerda?
Que te busquen en mi frente.
Juego de luna y arena.

|◀ ■ ▶ ‖ ● ▶|

So far I've argued that the Queerness of *Gypsy Ballads* reveals itself through subversion but also through a utopian aesthetic. Where, then, is the connection between Queerness as aesthetic and Queerness as sexuality? Certainly, I do not aim to completely dislocate the term 'Queer' from the realm of gender and sexuality. Rather I want to situate the homoeroticism of Lorca's work into a broader landscape of Queerness. Take this stanza from Lorca's poem *San Miguel*:

> *Saint Michael full of laces*
> *in the bedroom of his tower*
> *Shows his beautiful thighs*
> *encircled by lanterns*

It's hardly breaking news that Lorca was gay, and many of his works have been interpreted to tease out its homoerotic themes. However, I have yet to encounter an interpretation of *Gypsy Ballads* that goes beyond simply identifying and decoding homoerotic language. We can count and recount the number of times Lorca artfully employs the word *virile*, a scantily clad Saint and a *sword of lilies* but this doesn't go far toward investigating what these images are actually doing in the work. *Saint Michael* does more than only titillate the reader; the poem also fulfills the author's deepest obsessions. Lorca's words and images contribute

to the creation of another world, a utopia, in which fulfill-
ment of such divergent fantasies are possible.

Saint Michael (Granada)

by Federico García Lorca
(translation by Olive Esther Kuhn)

Visible from the verandas
of the hills, the hills, the hills,
mules and the shadows of mules
carry sunflowers on their backs.

Their eyes in the dark spaces
are filled with immense night.
In the swirling air crackles
a salty sunrise.

A heaven of white mules
closes its quicksilver eyes
lending the quiet half-
light a finale of hearts.

And the water grows cold
so that no one will touch it.
Crazy, uncovered water by
the hill, the hill, the hill.

Saint Michael full of laces
in the bedroom of his tower
Shows his beautiful thighs
encircled by lanterns.

Domesticated Archangel
in the shape of the Twelve
sweetly feigns a fury
of nightingales and feathers.
Saint Michael sings in the windows;

an ephebe of three thousand nights,
smelling of eau de cologne
and far away from the flowers.

By the beach the sea dances
a poem of balconies.
The shores of the moon
lose grasses, gain voices.

The women come, eating
sunflower seeds, with their
enormous, covered behinds
like planets of copper.
Tall horseback riders come,
and women of sad comportment
darkened by a nostalgia
for a past of nightingales.
And the bishop of Manila
blinded by saffron and poor,
says mass before a double-edged line
for women and for men.

Saint Michael was quiet
in his tower bedroom.
His underskirt gilded
with threads and tiny mirrors.

Saint Michael, king of the spheres
and monarch of odd numbers,
dressed in the finest berber attire
of crying and verandas.

|◄ ■ ► || ● ►|

Losing Lorca: a mixtape critique

San Miguel (Granada)
by Federico García Lorca

Se ven desde las barandas
de la monte, monte, monte,
mulos y sombras de mulos
cargados de girasoles.

Sus ojos en las umbrías
se empañan de inmensa noche.
En los recodos del aire,
cruje la aurora salobre.

Un cielo de mulos blancos
cierra sus ojos de azogue
dando a la quieta penumbra
un final de corazones.

Y el agua se pone fría
para que nadie la toque.
Agua loca y descubierta
por el monte, monte, monte.

San Miguel, llena de encajes
en la alcoba de su torre,
enseña sus bellos muslos
ceñidos por los faroles.
Arcángel domesticado
en el gesto de las doce,
finge una cólera dulce
de plumas y ruiseñores.
San Miguel canta en los vidrios;
efebo de tres mil noches,
fragrante de agua colonia
y lejano de las flores.

El mar baila por la playa
un poema de balcones.

Las orillas de la luna
pierden juncos, ganan voces.
Vienen manolas comiendo
semillas de girasoles,
los culos grandes y ocultos,
como planetas de cobre.
Vienen altos caballeros
y damas de triste porte,
morenas por la nostalgia
de un ayer de ruiseñores.
Y el obispo de Manila,
ciego de azafrán y pobre,
dice misa con dos filos
para mujeres y hombres.

San Miguel se estaba quieto
en la alcoba de su torre
con las enaguas cuajadas
de espejitos y entredoses.

San Miguel, rey de los globos
y de los números nones,
en el primer berberisco
de gritos y miradores.

|◄◄ ■ ► II ● ►►|

In *San Miguel*, Lorca describes a procession of horses, women and men moving en masse up the tower of the salacious Saint Michael. I can't presume to know of Federiquito's personal appetites, but I like to imagine in this poem he is codifying his sexual fantasies in a kind of strange inversion of a Catholic pilgrimage. In Lorca's Queer utopian gaze, male-on-male desire is not just allowed, it's holy.

SIDE B:

Translating duende

SUGGESTED TRACKS:

01. *Look Into My Eyes*, Janelle Monáe
02. *Last Goodbye*, Jeff Buckley
03. *Di mi nombre*, Rosalía
04. *The Body is a Blade*, Japanese Breakfast
05. *Sneakers*, Palehound
06. *Death Comes In Three*, Tica Douglas
07. *Taza de Café*, Ani Cordero
08. *Material Girl*, Madonna
09. *Take Ecstasy With Me*, The Magnetic Fields

First Green

by Olive Esther Kuhn

I read that 'having a coke with you' poem again,
and I thought of you smashing the glass bottle
against the side of the cafe table
and holding the sea green shard to my throat.

So I retreat into the sweaty sheets,
the sting of predictable nightmares,
the 8am alarm.

But my confessions are small, petty things
that flock like flies to your light.

Nightmare number one you run me through
with the shattered coke bottle I throw you over
the balcony of a moving ship.

Nightmare number two I kiss you
in public a glass breaks
in your mother's hand.

⏮ ■ ▶ ⏸ ● ⏭

Second Green

by Olive Esther Kuhn

The colors stain your fingers
and it is a green summer.

I stop thinking, to claw out
space for your voice in my brain

I do not write. I am not blocked.
I am the block.

The moon collides with my back
and does not enter the room.

I cannot see you.
I love you too much.

The sentiment pollutes you and
you swat it away from your face.

Your hand moves like a bird through mist
and disappears into the swarm

of my lust, which is light green
like basil, or a mint plant's stem,

or another pretty, bitter thing
that tastes bad on its own.

⏮ ⏹ ▶ ⏸ ⏺ ⏭

I wrote these two poems in response to Lorca's
*Sleepwalker Ballad, (Green how I want you green, green
the wind, green the moon, green my left nipple, etc.)* Part
of my process was to translate each ballad three times.
The first version adhered to a strict metrical scheme, the

second was more impressionistic and the third is simply my own dialogue with Lorca. This process is not fully evident in the final format of this book, but it was integral in producing the poems I chose to include. In this case, *First Green* and *Second Green* are actually my third "translations" of *Sleepwalker Ballad*. One of my objectives in this process was to suggest a methodology of Queer translation. I wanted to take the act of translation and Queer it. Rather than think about translation as a process which yields a useful product, I wanted to think of translation as a joyful and experimental process.

In the chapter *Feeling Utopia* of *Cruising Utopia: the then and now of queer futurity*, Muñoz provides a reading of Frank O'Hara's poem *Having a Coke with You.* What makes the poem Queer, to Muñoz, is not just O'Hara's sexuality but rather the way in which O'Hara takes the prosaic act of drinking a Coke and renders it poetic. Peering through the green glass bottle, O'Hara finds his lover, refracted and incandescent. The image subsumes a consumerist landscape into a new (or ancient) glistening world. The drink is both transformational and transformed, and this is the source (or symptom) of its Queerness.

I think of translation as a functional act, similar to how drinking a soda is a functional act. When I say that I want to write Queer translation, I mean that I want to transform the act of translation from merely functional into something revelatory in the same way O'Hara transformed the act of having a Coke. By transforming this process, the process transforms itself.

And yet, as is true of any transformation, something is lost. Burn a candle for light, and half the light escapes as heat. To even the most accomplished translator (which I am far from), hauling a piece of writing from one language into another is a mournful game, a game of leaving things behind. You're walking a significant distance and you can't carry everything with you. The walk is beautiful and you love everything you carry, but you keep dropping breadcrumbs. A double-entendre, a rhyme, a particularly beautiful word: we can't take all our friends along with us.

In my experience, being Queer feels similar. Even today, amid another year of corporate sponsored Pride Marches and endless advertising which divergently sells our own bodies back to us, (I am using the second person recklessly, I know) we are tasked with reclaiming our identities. Our very language is sewn together from rescued slurs. Reclaim the word Queer, reclaim the word Gay, reclaim Stonewall, reclaim Pride from cop cars decked out in rainbows, reclaim Queer politics from Pete Buttigieg's wine cave...you get the idea? My point is that you can't reclaim something unless it was once stolen from you.

The sense of loss inherent to Queerness is ontological, historical, and political. I don't need to tell you about the AIDS crisis and how it is not over. I don't need to tell you that twenty-six trans women were confirmed murdered in 2019 (which means this is probably an undercount). I don't need to tell you that, when I was researching Muñoz's work, I reached out to a professor who knew him personally; the professor kindly responded to my email saying that his memories of Muñoz were still too raw, too painful, to be discussed between teacher and student.

Federico García Lorca was executed by the Spanish Civil Guard on August 18, 1936. He was thirty-eight years old. José Esteban Muñoz died of heart failure in New York City on December 3, 2013. He was forty-six years old. I was far into this project before it occurred to me that in mooring Lorca's *Gypsy Ballads* (1928) to Munoz's *Cruising Utopia...* (2009), I was perhaps writing yet another Queer tragedy. How can it be, even among utopians, that death is everywhere? This is not a productive question. Better said: how can one write about utopia when the reality of history is permeated by the smell of death? How can I translate these ballads without reading young Antoñito's death as an omen of Lorca's demise? How can one read *Cruising Utopia...* without crying? In order to preserve the ludic and lyrical sense of *Gypsy Ballads*, I decided I had to altogether "forget" Lorca's execution. Yet in so many ways, the historical weight of Lorca's death seems to outlive him.

Arrest Of Antoñito el Camborio On Way To Seville

by Federico García Lorca
(translation by Olive Esther Kuhn)

Antonio Torres Heredia
son and grandson of the Camborios,
with a wooden staff in hand,
walks to Seville to see the bulls
Swarthy like a young moon,
his walk is slow and confident.
His perfumed curls fall gleaming
in between his eyes.
Halfway down the path, he cut
round lemons from the trees,
and went throwing them in the river
until it began to turn gold.
And halfway down the path,
beneath the branches of an elm tree,
the Civil Guard, who were passing by,
took him away by the elbows.

The day progresses slowly;
the afternoon, hung from one shoulder,
sweeps its torero's cape
over the sea and its shores.
The olive trees stand guard
over the Capricorn night
and a little breeze, on horseback,
leaps over the leaden mountains.

Antonio Torres Heredia
son and grandson of the Camborios
comes without his wooden staff
surrounded by five tricorn hats.

Antoñito, who are you?
If you called yourself a Camborio
by now you'd have cut a fountain
of blood with five open spouts.

No, you are a son of no one,
no legitimate Camborio.
They've killed off all the gypsies
that traveled the hills alone!
Their old knives shake
beneath this dust.

At nine o'clock in the evening
they bring him to the dungeon
while all the civil guards
drink lemonade together.
And at nine o'clock in the evening
they close the doors to the dungeon
while the night sky shines
like the rump of a foal.

◄◄ ■ ► ❙❙ ● ►►❙

Prendimiento de Antoñito el Camborio En El Camino de Sevilla
by Federico García Lorca

Antonio Torres Heredia,
hijo y nieto de Camborios,
con una vara de mimbre
va a Sevilla a ver los toros.
Moreno de verde luna
anda despacio y garboso.
Sus empavonados bucles
le brillan entre los ojos.
A la mitad del camino
cortó limones redondos,
y los fue tirando al agua
hasta que la puso de oro.
Y a la mitad del camino,
bajo las ramas de un olmo,
guardia civil caminera
lo llevó codo con codo.

El día se va despacio,
la tarde colgada a un hombro,
dando una larga torera
sobre el mar y los arroyos.
Las aceitunas aguardan
la noche de Capricornio,
y una corta brisa, ecuestre,
salta los montes de plomo.
Antonio Torres Heredia,
hijo y nieto de Camborios,
viene sin vara de mimbre
entre los cinco tricornios.

Antonio, ¿quién eres tú?
Si te llamaras Camborio,
hubieras hecho una fuente
de sangre con cinco chorros.
Ni tú eres hijo de nadie,
ni legítimo Camborio.
¡Se acabaron los gitanos
que iban por el monte solos!
Están los viejos cuchillos
tiritando bajo el polvo.

A las nueve de la noche
lo llevan al calabozo,
mientras los guardias civiles
beben limonada todos.
Y a las nueve de la noche
le cierran el calabozo,
mientras el cielo reluce
como la grupa de un potro.

⏮ ■ ▶ ‖ ● ⏭

Olive Esther Kuhn

Death Of Antoñito el Camborio

by Federico García Lorca
(translation by Olive Esther Kuhn)

Voices of death resounded
along the Guadalquivir.
Ancient voices encircle
his virile carnation voice.
He struck upwards in an arc
from their boots with a boar's tusk.
In the fight he dove and dealt
Slippery blows like a dolphin.
His already-crimson necktie
bathed in his enemies' blood
But they fought with the force of four
knives, and so he succumbed.

When the stars drive iron nails
into the clouded water,
When veronica flowers
dance in the dreams of young bulls,
voices of death resounded
along the Guadalquivir.
Antonio Torres Heredia
The thick-haired Camborio,
swarthy beneath a green moon,
voice of a virile carnation:
Who has robbed you of your life
along the Guadalquivir?
My four cousins Heredias
The sons of Benamejí.
that which others envied not,
they did envy in me.
Maroon shoes, ivory lockets,
and this skin, massaged
with oils and with jazmine.

Ay, Antoñito el Camborio,
deserving of an empress!
think back upon the Virgin
for you are going to die.
Ay, Federico García,
summon the civil guard!
My body has snapped in half
at the waist like a stalk of corn.
They struck him three bloody blows
and he died in silhouette.
A living rare coin who, once
lost, will not be seen again.

An overzealous angel
lays his head on a cushion.
Others, flushed with exhaustion,
set flame within a lamp.
and when the four Heredias
arrived at Benameji,
voices of death ceased to sound
along the Guadalquivir.

|◀◀ ■ ▶ ‖ ● ▶▶|

Muerte de Antoñito el Camborio
by Federico García Lorca

Voces de muerte sonaron
cerca de Guadalquivir.
Voces antiguas que cercan
voz de clavel varonil.
Les clavó sobre las botas
mordiscos de jabalí.
En la lucha daba saltos
jabonados de delfín.
Baño con sangre enemiga
su corbata carmesí.

Pero eran cuatro puñales
y tuvo que sucumbir.
Cuando las estrellas claven
rejones el agua gris,
cuando los erales sueñan
verónicas de alhelí,
voces de muerte sonaron
cerca del Guadalquivir.

Antonio Torres Heredia
Camborio de dura crin,
moreno de verde luna,
voz de clavel varonil:
¿Quién te ha quitado la vida
cerca de Guadalquivir?
Mis cuatros primos Heredias
hijos de Benamejí.
Lo que en otros no envidiaban,
ya lo envidiaban en mí.
Zapatos color corinto,
medallones de marfil,
y este cutis amasado
con aceituna y jazmín.
¡Ay, Antoñito el Camborio
digno de una Emperatriz!
Acuérdate de la vírgen,
porque te vas a morir.
¡Ay, Federico García,
llama a la Guardia Civil!
Ya mi talle se ha quebrado
como caña de maíz.
Tres golpes de sangre tuvo
y se murió de perfil.
Viva moneda que nunca
se volverá a repetir.
Un ángel marchoso pone
su cabeza en un cojín.
Otros de rubor cansado
encendieron un candil.

Y cuando los cuatro primos
llegan a Benamejí,
voces de muerte cesaron
cerca de Guadalquivir.

|◀ ■ ▶ || ● ▶|

For Elizabeth Bishop
by Olive Esther Kuhn

Please come flying
over the burning
places the holes
dug into now
domestic flatland
the witch's body
tomorrow's ravine
a thorned discourse
she says with perfect
horse's teeth, ignore
the lisp, ignore the smell
of death on the highway
death all up
in the tuberose petals death
on lugubrious April's breath.
Please come flying
out of the year
and into the shower
the gaudy pink
and into the shadow
the godly pink
the fucked up drain results
in overflow, bubble
calamity, call the landlord
drench all the towels
open the windows
a scream in the wind

an invented language
tomorrow, tonight
a light before
the tunnel even
begins.

⏮ ■ ▶ ‖ ● ⏭

To address the salient questions of Queerness in re-
lation to tragedy and death, I invoke (not without some
desperation) *duende*. The concept of *duende* haunted
Lorca's creative life from start to finish. The word, which
translates literally to goblin, refers to a certain zeitgeist, a
certain *je ne sais quoi*, that characterizes Flamenco, Cante
Jondo, and other Gitano/Andalusian art forms.

I feel that both Queerness and *duende* describe a
moment of crossing over and moving beyond, be it the
Brooklyn Bridge or death's threshold, In the final chapter
of *Cruising Utopia...* , Muñoz delves into Elizabeth Bishop's *Invitation to Miss Marianne Moore* to find the Queer
poetess inviting her companion to cross over the Brooklyn
Bridge. In a sense, *Invitation to Miss Marianne Moore* is
analogous to Lorca's *Ode to Salvador Dalí*. In terms of tone,
the poems are not even distantly related; Bishop writes
in free verse and inverted syntax, while Lorca writes in a
flowery iambic hexameter. Even so, both poems are poi-
gnant remnants of a love thwarted. Both are love poems by
well known artists directed at another well known artist.
And in both cases, the authors were later spurned by their
addressees.

Why would a utopian, such as Muñoz, spend precious time digging up the bones of a centuries old romance? The obvious answer is that linear time is fiction.
Another answer is such intertextual correspondence presents opportunities for the author to inhabit the dolorous
present with reparative texts (as I attempted to do in my
letter to Dalí).

Let me put it another way: have you ever looked at

photographs of the ashen bodies frozen in time at Mount Vesuvius, and imagined them as living people with flesh, hair and clothing? Have you ever tried to hold a conversation with one of them? Ask them how their day was, tell them about the most delicious thing you ate this week? It's a practice that I highly recommend.

You wouldn't guess it, but I wrote *For Elizabeth Bishop* as a companion to *Ballad of the Spanish Civil Guard*. Something about the plaintive refrain *please come flying* resonated in my psyche with Lorca's requiem for *a city of ache and musk*. Hope and mourning intersect. The death of the Queer city is only temporary. The Civil Guard burns the gypsy encampment to the ground; Marianne Moore and Elizabeth Bishop fly through the ashes holding hands.

THE CAMERA SAYS

Before working on Lorca's *Romancero Gitano*, I translated parts of Pedro Lemebel's *Loco Afán* (1996), a blistering account of the AIDS epidemic in Santiago, Chile. In *Loco Afán*, Lemebel Queers the Spanish language to a breaking point to deliver a series of chronicles, poems, and manifestos that take the reader on a vertiginous tour of personal and collective memories. Crafting translations of *Loco Afán* felt important to me for two reasons. First, there is no full English translation widely available. Second, the stories told in *Loco Afán* are likely not told elsewhere. History isn't the word; better said, a processional. Walk Lemebel's stone path of words, walk them on your knees.

Unlike that of Lemebel, Lorca's work is widely available in English, and multiple biographies tell his story. Yet throughout this project, reading and writing about Lorca and his life felt urgent to me. No matter how many biographies I read, no matter how many times we've searched for Lorca's unmarked grave, something remains to be said. Attention must be paid.

What happened to Lorca is not history, it is recursive reality. We can endlessly reframe history through a Queer lens or a Marxist lens or an anti-imperialist lens. But the camera takes the picture, not the lens. And the camera says that Franco's nationalism swallowed Catalonia. The camera says we lost Lorca not in an isolated tragedy but in a stream of state-sanctioned deaths. The camera says the *falangistas* hated fags, hated women, hated gypsies, hated black people, hated socialists, hated the working class, and above all hated solidarity.

The camera also says Vox, Spain's 'new' nationalist party, won 52 seats in lower parliament in 20–Fucking–19! This marks the first time since Franco's death in 1975 that a nationalist party has gained traction in the country. I've never been to Spain, but this seems to me like a bad thing.

As for the United States, let's shed some light on our recent past; the camera says capitalism stuck its head up its own anus and spat out Trump. The camera says the Democratic party is licking Joe Biden's asshole again. The camera says again and again and again and again. The camera says human bones are the last part of us to decompose.

Listen to Federico García Lorca's bones. Give or take a few inches, his skeleton is indistinguishable from yours or mine. So open your eyes and fight back.

ACKNOWLEDGEMENTS

In loving gratitude, the author would like to cite the works by Federico García Lorca, now in the public domain, that inspired this project to come to fruition:

El Publico
Oda A Salvador Dalí
Romancero Gitano
Romance Sonámbulo
Romance de la Guardia Civil de España
San Miguel (Granada)
Prendimiento de Antoñito el Camborio En El Camino de Sevilla
Muerte de Antoñito el Camborio

The author also gives a shout out to the following works and authors. Please inquire further at your local library or bookstore:

The Generation of 27
Cruising Utopia: the then and now of queer futurity by Jose Esteban Muñoz
Having a Coke with You by Frank O'Hara
Invitation to Miss Marianne Moore by Elizabeth Bishop
Loco Afán by Pedro Lemebel

SPECIAL THANKS

Thank you to my family for supporting me in the relatively tumultuous six years since I flew the coop.

Thank you to the staff at various Philadelphia coffee shops for blessing me with free refills as I sat and wrote for hours.

Thank you to my community of friends for holding my hand as I literally and metaphorically cried in an Applebee's.

Thank you to my undergraduate advisory board for helping me hatch the first iteration of this project.

Thank you to Christian for investing so much time and energy in this crazy endeavor.

Thank you to Bug for being the best little dude.

ABOUT THE AUTHOR

Olive Esther Kuhn is a Philadelphia-based writer and organizer originally from Middletown, CT. A recent graduate from Bard College where they studied Creative Writing, Poetry and Spanish, their work has appeared in *La Voz* magazine, *yst* publications, *Sui Generis*, *Bard Papers*, and *The Humanist* magazine. They have published two chapbooks of poetry: *A Bouquet of Roots* (2017) by the Bard Student Reading Series, and *Pink Telemachus* (2019), a poetic and visual collaboration with the artist Olivia Caro. They have read poetry at *The College Unions Poetry Slam International* (CUPSI) as well as many other poetry venues in NY and PA. Olive writes and performs their music under the name *Recluse Spider*. They are an active member of the international organization *Socialist Alternative*. In their free time Olive enjoys to cook, dance, spend quality time with friends, karaoke, reality television, crossword puzzles, and time with their twenty-one pound cat Bug.

This book & other
great work
available
at

www.rectoyverso.com